A LEGEND AMONG US

The Story of WILLIAM "Youngblood" "Bill" McCRARY

(Nicknamed "Youngblood" by Satchel Paige)

of the **NEGRO BASEBALL LEAGUE**

KANSAS CITY MONARCHS

LINDA PENNINGTON BLACK

William L. McCrary, Storyteller
Cover created by: Jessica Richardson
Professionally edited by: Alisia Compton
Photos provided by: William L. McCrary; unless otherwise noted.
Satchel Paige photo front cover by: Negro baseball eMuseum

Other books by author:
The Adventures of Boots: The Giant Snowball
A Porpoise for Cara
S.T.O.P. Bullying
My Daddy is a Star
Black also has a poem titled: **I Hear the Cry for Freedom,** published in the anthology: **Sistahs with Ink Voices,** and another titled**: The Dream/The Victory**, which was accepted by President Obama in 2008 for his first inauguration.

TABLE OF CONTENTS

Acknowledgements

I would like to express my sincere appreciation to Rowe and Patty Huggins, who consistently encouraged me to write this book. Rowe went as far as to say, "If you don't write it, somebody will, so you need to get on it."

My appreciation is extended to the many friends and family who took the time to write excerpts for the book. You added an extra special personal touch to it.

To William "Bill" McCrary, I respect and thank you for allowing me the opportunity to delve into his private life in order to write his story. For this I am grateful, in part for the wealth of knowledge I gained in the research, and alternatively, the discovery of a family member, Arthur "Superman" Pennington, who also played with the Negro Baseball League, and whom (before beginning work on this publication) I knew nothing about.

Last but not least, I respectfully extend my gratitude to Mr. Bob Kendrick, President of the Negro Baseball League Museum, for humbly accepting my request to write the foreword for this book. I asked, he responded, not "Maybe" or "I'll think about it," but "Absolutely." He said, "I'm honored," but Mr. Kendrick, it is I who am honored, and I appreciate your confidence in me.

Foreword

The story of the Negro Leagues is one of sheer determination and devotion. Strong-willed, dedicated athletes, who simply refused to accept the notion that they were unfit to share in the joys of our national pastime. They were baseball players first and foremost, who forged a glorious history during an inglorious era of American segregation.

But, the real story of the Negro Leagues is not about the adversity the players faced, but rather what they did to overcome that adversity. These talented athletes didn't cry about the social injustice they went out and did something about it. And, it's all based on one simple principle: *You won't let us play with you; then we'll create a league of our own.*

In 1920, Andrew "Rube" Foster founded the Negro Leagues in a meeting that took place at the Paseo YMCA in Kansas City, MO. The Negro Leagues would then provide a playing field for the best Black and Hispanic athletes to showcase their world class baseball skills. The Negro Leagues would operate for 40 years.

Stars were born. There's "Cool Papa" Bell, still believed to be the fastest man to ever play the game. He could circle the bases in 12 seconds. Or, the legendary Satchel Paige, who in 1948 became the oldest rookie in Major League Baseball history at the tender age of 42. Or was it 52? Only Satch knew...and he never told.

By the time the dust settled more than 2,600 men and women had played in the Negro Leagues. William McCrary was in that number. Signed by the

Kansas City Monarchs when he was just 17, the talented Beloit, Wisconsin native more than held his own competing against men twice his age. In these pages you'll get to meet the man dubbed "Youngblood" by Satchel.

His story embodies everything that made the Negro Leagues special. He was a talented athlete, a great family man, devoted husband and has dedicated much of his life to helping others.

I consider myself fortunate to have gotten to know "Youngblood" during my tenure at the Negro Leagues Baseball Museum (NLBM). The NLBM is dedicated to ensuring that America's unsung baseball heroes will never be forgotten. It's more than a cultural facility that just chronicles history, it inspires. The NLBM conveys the human struggle while demonstrating the power of the human spirit to overcome those challenges.

"Youngblood" McCrary is rightfully proud of his stint in the Negro Leagues. He should be. We are equally proud of him and for his selflessness, dedication, courage and perseverance. He was part of a team that took the field with great pride and an even greater resolve. As a result, they changed America's pastime and America too!

Bob Kendrick,
President
Negro Leagues Baseball Museum
Kansas City, MO

Chapter 1: A Brief History of Blacks in Baseball

Most people today will never lay eyes on a great legend of the Negro Baseball League because the league dates as far back as the 1800s, and the last games were played in the early 1960s; meaning: even the youngest players have aged passed retirement.

If you ever did find yourself in the company of one, what would you say? What would you do or ask? You'd have a lot of questions, and truthfully the answers would vary depending on who you were speaking with, but one fact remains: most answers will not be so different when the question is about the ballplayers of the Negro teams during the era. The names of teams and players don't change, and they remain forever legends; both in the annals of history, but also in the souls of the players who still exist to tell their tales.

In the 1800s, Blacks played baseball in college, and on Military and company teams. Some even played baseball professionally. The first known Black professional league player, to participate on an integrated, team was Bud Fowler. He is considered a pioneer of Black baseball, and has played on countless teams. Moses Fleetwood "Fleet" Walker, of the minor league team Toledo Blue Stockings, was one of the first African Americans to play on an integrated professional major league team. *Or was he?*

The name William Edward White (who played a single game with the Providence Grays) is flaunted as being the first Black in integrated major league history. There is very limited information on White, including very inconclusive information in regards to his baseball career. Why is it that nobody knows anything about this man of early baseball? Is it because he passed for white? That's what his birth certificate read. He is said to have been born of a slave master and one of his slaves, who was mulatto. He took the name of his father, the master, and was sent north, henceforth to live as a white man. Very little is known about him, so will we ever know who the "first" was truly?

On August 10, 1883, the Chicago White Stockings, led by Adrian "Cap" Anson, refused to play in an exhibition game (against the Toledo Blue Stockings) because Moses Fleetwood "Fleet" Walker was playing. Upon the insistence of the Blue Stockings manager that the game be played, Anson gave in.

In 1887, Anson again objected when George Stovey, the country's first African-American pitcher, was to pitch in a game against the Chicago White Stockings.

Walker became the first Black major league player when the Blue Stockings joined the American Association in 1884. When the

International League banned any future contracts with Black players in 1887, many were forced from their teams and excluded from playing, although those who already had contracts were allowed to continue with their teams. With the inception of racist "Jim Crow" laws, and the game segregations instigated by Cap Anson, professional baseball would remain divided for almost 60 years, until late in the 1940s.

Pictured: First Colored World Series; Kansas City, Mo. Library of Congress Prints and Photographs Division, Washington, D.C. 20540 SA;httphdl.loc.govloc.pnpcph.3c32218.

The opening game on October 11th, 1924

Pictured: African American baseball players from Morris Brown College; Atlanta, Georgia httphdl.loc.govloc.pnpcph.3c14266

Players relax for a group photo. A sharp-dressed man leans against a door, while another man holds a small child in his lap

Pictured: Bud Fowler; Baseball Hall of Fame; Library
Cooperstown, NY D31299

Pictured: Moses Fleetwood Walker

Andrew "Rube" Foster was a former player, manager and owner of the Chicago American Giants. He led the orchestration and organization of the union that became known as, "The Negro National League in 1920," at the Paseo YMCA in Kansas City. Many looked at it as a "semipro" or "sandlot" league, but it essentially had the two main components of a Major League: a world series and an all-star game called The East-West Game.

Pictured: Rube Foster

Photos courtesy of Negro League Baseball Museum

East West All-Stars

Rube Foster's Chicago American Giants

Soon, with the birth of this league, came rival establishments from other areas of the country, such as Canada and Latin America, to challenge and to bring economic progress to many Black communities, both urban and rural Black ball players were among the best players around, but they couldn't play in the Major League because of the "Jim

Crow" laws, and rights that were reserved exclusively for whites; however, they remained as proud and as athletic as their white counterparts. Great baseball players have graced the cow pastures, the dirt fields, and the alleyways of many venues for the love of the game, but very few have been acknowledged for their greatness.

Names such as Satchel Paige, Jackie Robinson, Ernie Banks, Roy Campanella, Willie Mays and Hank Aaron hit the airwaves, but they are only a drop in the bucket. There are so many more outstanding Black players who had high hopes of finding their names in the headlines, but rarely did. Although these men were considered the best of the best, others, such as Buck O'Neil, "Cool Papa" Bell, Josh Gibson, "Rube" Foster, "Mule" Suttles, and many others (who had great skills and gave their all, with many contributions to the league), never made it to the big league. Most of these players were either too old to play or passed away by the time Negroes were considered to play the majors, leaving a legacy of unanswered dreams and shattered hopes.

Satchel Paige said, "In the late Thirties, any Negro League club could have beaten any white major league team. The best team in the world was the New York Yankees then, and if we played them with the Crawford's or Gray's, they'd have had to go like hell to beat us."

These great men and women of baseball brought enormous professionalism and original styles, frills and thrills to the many rural and urban communities across the country, north and south, east and west, including Latin America.

Most people probably don't realize there were three women who played with the men in the Negro Baseball League. Toni Stone (Marceni Lyle Stone Alberga) was an accomplished athlete from Minneapolis, and she was contracted to play second base in 1953, and replaced Hank Aaron when Aaron left the Indianapolis Clowns for the majors. Mamie "Peanuts" Johnson, a right-hand pitcher from Washington D.C., was the second female signed to pitch for the Clowns. Connie Morgan, from Philadelphia, was the third woman to sign a Negro Leagues contract when Toni Stone was traded in 1954 to the Kansas City Monarchs.

The historic signing of the first African American, Jackie Robinson, to the Major League, and the recruiting of the best Black players, brought a turning point in Civil Rights history and the decline of the Negro Leagues. In 1948, the Negro National League held their last game. After that the Negro American League is the only African American league still in force. By 1952, with low attendance and lack of good players, it further declined. The era of Negro League baseball drew to an end, with the last integrations occurring in 1959. So many African American players had already integrated to the majors, leaving only the last Negro League teams to dry up: the Detroit-New Orleans Stars, the Kansas City Monarchs, the Raleigh Tigers and the Birmingham Black Barons. The historic Negro Leagues were finished for good.

Because of their triumphs and difficulties, and because they deserve their place in the annals of history, it is my solemn dedication to bring to the forefront the endowments of these great men and women of the forgotten Negro Baseball League by recounting one man's story.

Chapter 2: Where it All Began For One Man

Beloit is a small community in Wisconsin, nestled along a river, with many spectacular characteristics, including beautiful tree-lined streets. It prides itself on its rich culture and heritage; its production and progress.

Located approximately nineteen miles north of Rockford, Illinois, Beloit lies just across the Wisconsin-Illinois state line from South Beloit, Illinois, which is part of the Rockford area.

Once a thriving town of leading manufacturers, it has seen its ups and downs, progressions and setbacks. The town boasts the moniker, *The Gem of the Rock River Valley*, aptly nicknamed for the river it is situated along. It has in its fingerprint the only city in Rock County to be given The All-America Award, the oldest community recognition program in the nation, and the only city in the state of Wisconsin to be home to three multi-billion dollar international companies: ABC Supply Company, Regal-Beloit, and Kerry Ingredients.

Unbeknownst to many, a legend was born in the city of Beloit on November 5, 1929; a young boy who would later set his sights on the dream of a lifetime: to play in the major leagues. With a bat in one hand,

and a ball in the other, he rose up the ranks, as one of the best Negro baseball players around.

Bill remembers, "Lots of the Black people lived in an apartment building called: Edgewater Flats; the factory Fairbanks and Morris built for their employees. Each building had six apartments, and the baseball field, called 'Grady Field' (after the man who owned it and the manager of the ball team). Grady Field was the field Black ballplayers used, and it was located just behind the apartment building. I lived in Apartment 2."

He remembers some of the players who played with the team, "The Flats Team: Pat Kenny, Jerry Kenny and Pete Edwards."

Chapter 3: Family life, Early Childhood and School

When asked about his family, Bill reminisces on the many facets of his life. He was born William Page, to Roy and Mettie Page. His mother died in childbirth with him. Today, a family portrait stands on the mantle of a fireplace in his home, and it is of his biological father and mother. It's the only visual he's ever had of his mother. He states, "I wish I had known her, but I had wonderful foster parents."

When he was just a youngster, Bill's name changed forever after he was nicknamed Bill, and people stopped calling him William.

The family (Joe, Frances, Steve George, Clifford, Wanda, and Bill and father Roy) tried moving on, but struggled to stay together. Bill was the youngest. Frances, his oldest sister, and his father did everything they could to take care of him, but it proved to be too much for a newly widowed working man, and such a young girl. His father had to work to make a living, and simply couldn't care for a young child.

A barren couple, Bud and Stella McCrary, had tried repeatedly to have children of their own, but all their efforts proved fruitless. They came to Roy, asking if they could raise Bill, who by that time was living at a school for fostered children. Roy knew the McCrary's very well, and he instantly agreed to the arrangement.

Pictured: Roy and Mettie Page

Bill's biological parents stand together in a photo he has to commemorate their relationship. His father holds a trumpet, and his mother holds out a chair, as if to her child. The photograph currently resides on Bill's fireplace mantle.

After I was married, I went to see my sister Frances who lived in Peoria, Illinois, and found out I had brothers and another sister. I had never heard of them, only Frances. She gave me my Brother Clifford's phone number.

He lived in Chicago. When I got home that night I called him. He asked me where I was and I told him in Maywood, where I lived at that time. He told me he would be right over. My other brother George lived in Ottawa, Illinois. I met him later. Wanda was the last one I met. She lived in Ottawa also, but now she lives in Chicago. She and I are the only ones left. Since we didn't grow up together, we weren't close. I haven't seen her in about two years, but we talk on the phone quite often.

I didn't know much about my biological family on either side, but I do remember traveling on the train somewhere to the south, with my foster father, to take the body of my biological father home to his family. I spotted a man on that train that had an unusually shaped head and turned to my father and said, "That man is akin to me." He asked, "Well how do you know that?" I said, "Look at his head." My father turned to me and said, "If he is related to you, he'll be going the same place we are going."

When we arrived, that man got off at the same stop. Later at my grandfather's home he was introduced as my father's brother. My grandfather was an old man and that was the first and only time I met him, but he lived to be one hundred and seven years old. I really enjoyed that visit, not under the circumstances, but to talk with him. He told me some stories, but none of which I still remember.

Pictured: Bill, Wanda, and Cliff

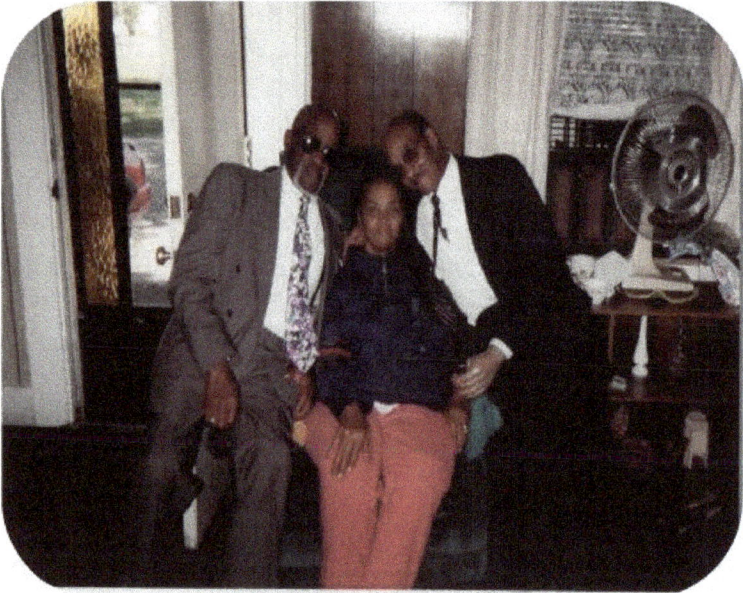

Pictured: Bill and Brother George

Roy never removed his arms from around his son. Although he wasn't being raised by him, Bill reiterates, "My father was always there attending all my ball games, and assisting in every decision about me. He didn't just give me away because he never let me go. He knew he couldn't properly raise me, so he let someone else do it, and the McCrary's were the perfect couple. They were wonderful parents. My foster father was something else. He was a great man. Unfortunately, I can't find any pictures of my foster parents."

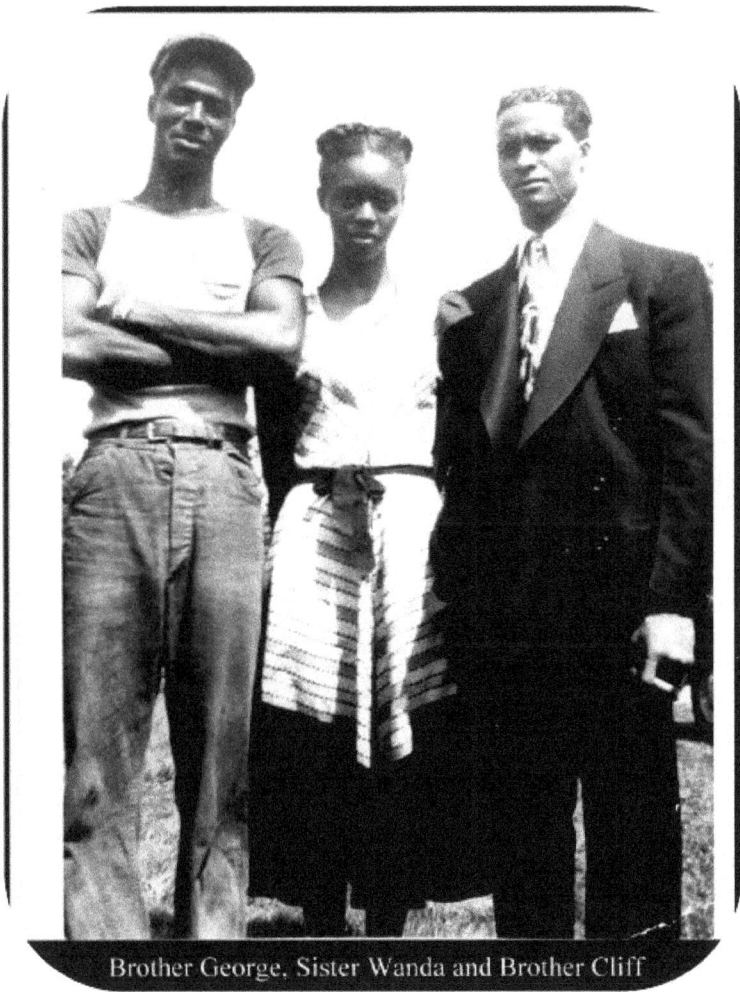

Brother George, Sister Wanda and Brother Cliff

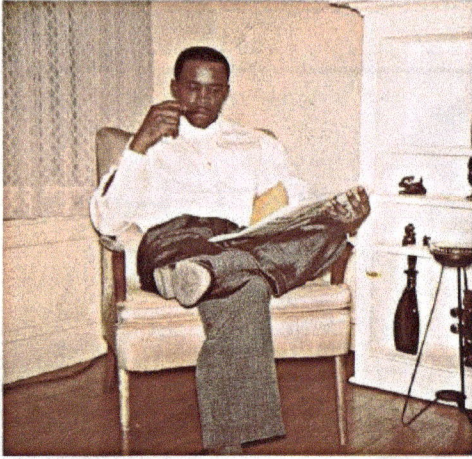
Bill relaxing at home

Francis

Son Tracy and his family

Pictured: A Letter to Papa

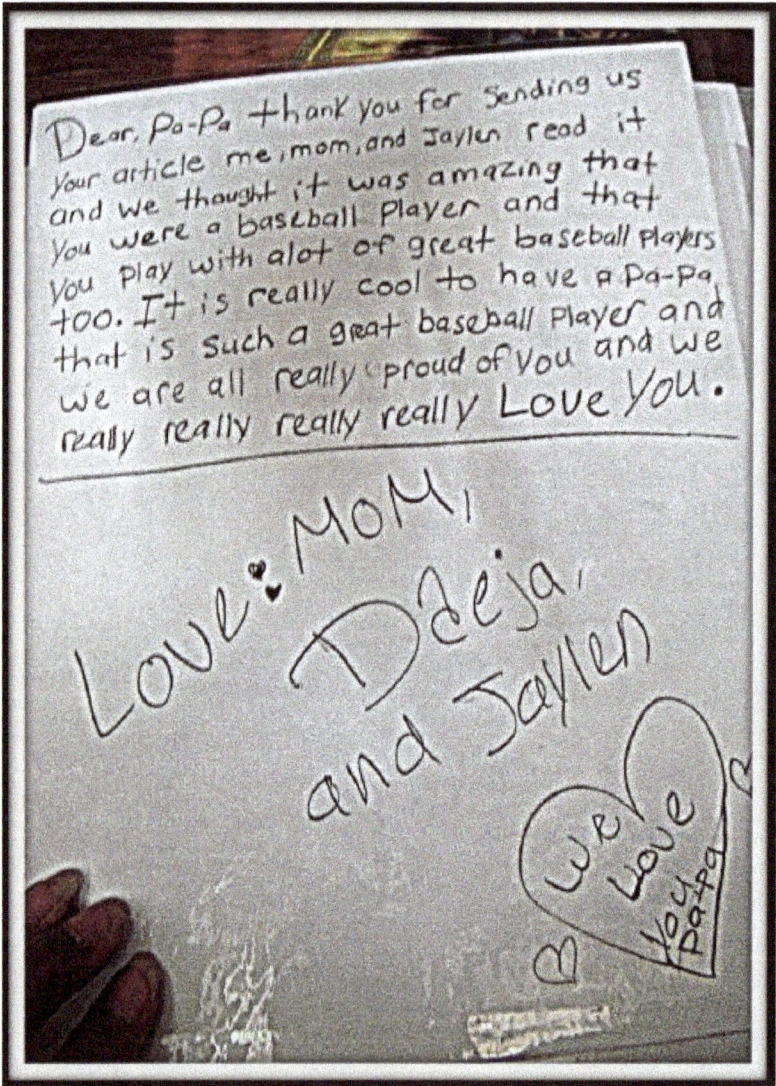

Bill and Tracy both agree that their relationship hasn't been a close one, until recent years. For personal family reasons they hadn't been able to connect, but both thank God every day that the bond between them is growing stronger and stronger with every passing day. Communication and understanding has reached new heights, and they are moving forward with their relationship, with the help of God in their lives. Both are very religious and God-fearing men.

Tracy sends love and warm wishes to his dad and reminds him that he will always be there for him:

When I try to do anything these days, I have to go to what I was taught, that being - putting God first in my life. Genesis 1:1 says, "In the beginning God (the foundation for all things to be)," and Proverbs 3:6 says, "In all thy ways acknowledge Him and He shall direct thy path."

God, being acknowledged, has brought our relationship (my dad and me) together, and putting Him first in our lives, we know it will be a continued success. Growing up, I was told about my dad's gift to play the game of baseball, which I also played. I often wondered how I would've fared against him, so I began to compare. Speed, I would've been faster; Fielding, we would've been about equal; Hitting, he was better (laugh), not by much, but the big edge was his resolve to make it.

If I had the determination he had, who knows, you may be writing about me today (chuckles). All in all, when God has a plan for you, you don't have to push; you just walk in the plan.

I love you dad!

Tracy Leroy.

Bill remarried Cleatrice "Cleo" in 1959. By then, he and Priscilla had long been apart. He reminisces on how they met and what close friends they were.

Every year, she would come to visit her brother in Beloit, who lived next door to my mother and my grandmother. I remember when she got married for the first time. She knew my wife and I knew her husband. I don't know if the loss of her son (in the accident where she was driving) affected her marriage or not. She was coming from visiting her mother in Fulton, MO. when she had the accident. Shortly after that she moved to Maywood, Illinois.

By then, we had become very good friends, so she called me one day and asked me to come visit. She was staying with a cousin. Meeting her cousin at the door, I told her who I was and who I had come to see. She asked me to take off my shoes before entering. I didn't know if I heard her right so I begged her pardon. She repeated for me to take off my shoes.

I told her just to tell Cleo that I was there and left. I didn't feel anyone's home was so precious that I had to remove my shoes before entering.

With his second marriage came a daughter, Linda, whom he adopted and raised as his own. Linda Grayson and her daughter, (Bill's granddaughter) Sakai, live in California.

Pictured above: Linda; Pictured below: Daughter Sakai

Linda's heartfelt sentiments to her dad:

When reflecting on my Dad, I have such an awesome feeling of pride! He has always had my back, believing, even when I was doubting myself. To listen to his stories of playing baseball was a usual occurrence at our home. It was like having our own guide thru Black History with little personal tidbits. I, his more militant and outspoken child, once wore his Kansas City Monarchs' uniform as a part of an 'Ancestral Run,' instead of getting caught up in Halloween. Little did I realize at the time, understand or appreciate the magnitude his contribution to Black History or the footprint he left.

He's such a proud, quiet man, but firmly committed to your betterment. Being someone you didn't want to disappoint because it meant 'getting the look,' I went to college and made the usual freshman call, 'I want to come home'. He very calmly told me, "fine, quit, come home, but you'll have to get a job and pay rent." Of course, that quaint nudge produced a college graduate in three years instead of four! Once again when I told him I was going to pursue a master's degree, but it would more than likely take three years because I was teaching full time. He said, "Fine, but I'll be there in two years." Yes, it was done in two years, with you-know-who sitting front and center.

Loving your Dad is a given, but respecting and honoring him is my own personal joy. He's really not judgmental, only shaking and rubbing his head in disbelief of my numerous foolish antics. When he met my daughter, his granddaughter, for the first time his comment was 'good job.' I knew at that moment she too would have all his love and support. She tried to be so much like her 'Grandpa', even played softball. Somehow the great baseball gene must have skipped her. Together, they would sit for hours watching baseball. He taught her how to bat, keep an official score sheet, sit and wait for a fish to bite, and how to bowl.

If we, his kids and grandkids, inherited nothing from Dad it's not just a love for the game, but to be calm, show a sense of humor, believe in a higher power and play the game of life with integrity and spunk!

The following is Sakai Bonds-McCrary's reflection on her Grandpa written by her:

There is an inherent biological relationship and emotional bonding between grandfather and granddaughter that comes only with effort. It happens when the granddaughter sees that you are open to forming a relationship. It happens when you get off your easy chair and make the time to see what matters to your granddaughter.

The smile on Grandpa's face is a lasting memory in my heart. Nothing in the world can keep us apart. He's the one who taught me how to ride a bike, fish, bowl, play cards, trips for shaved iced, and even let me sip his coffee. He knew what to say at the right time with the right tone. I'd like to say 'thank you' to my Grandpa; for being the best that he could be. You're my confidante and best friend. I believe you know how much I love you with all my heart. The happiness you've given me will last a lifetime.

Two of Bill's nieces (Brother Steve's children), Rosemary Clemmer and Elizabeth "Betty" Lampkin, have expressed their gratitude, appreciation, and well wishes. They don't use any form of social media, but their sentiments shall be known in this writing. Two other nieces (Brother Joe's daughters) also send their love and tribute.

Rosemary met him at the age of twelve, and he became a father figure to her. She had always been very close to Uncle Billy and Aunt Cleo before she passed away.

A note from Rosemary reads:

Uncle Billy, you know I love you and wish you well. I'm so happy you are finally getting your story out. I've loved you from the first day I met you at "Mother's" house (I called his sister

Francis, Mother, because she raised me, but he helped.) Mother never had children of her own but she raised many family members. I love you Uncle Billy.

Your Niece Rosemary

Betty was grown when she first met Bill, and they didn't have as much interaction as he and Rosemary; however, she did know him.

Betty expressed:

Uncle Billy I'm so happy you are getting your just notice and very thankful it came at a time where you can enjoy the acknowledgements. I love you!

Your niece, Elizabeth "Betty"

Love has no measure when it comes to family, and family isn't always blood, and this is especially true for Bill's extended family. He cherishes the relationship with each one. Each one has different roles in his life but the affection for each is the same. It comes unconditionally.

Along the way, he also gained a very special "adopted" daughter: Amy Thomason, and three godchildren: Jake Fisher in Florida, Elaine Brannon in Nevada, and Ida Cotton in Mississippi. An excerpt from an old friend, the Reverend Hadley Edwards of Louisiana, from back in Fulton Missouri is also included in this section.

A monumental recollection from Jake:

I returned to Chicago as a Vietnam Vet, in late December of 1967. I started attending a Jr. College in the City in January of 1968, and Martin Luther King was assassinated just a few months later. Robert Kennedy was assassinated shortly after that. Mayor Daley, the Chicago Police, and the hippies (who were protesting the Vietnam "conflict" in Grant Park) were fighting a very different kind of war.

Chicago was a mess, and there were race riots in almost every major city in America. I couldn't help but wonder, why I had even bothered to come back home.

I had no real family to speak of, although both of my parents lived in the Chicagoland area. I hadn't known my Father much as a kid growing up. My mother struggled trying to provide for her three kids, and

41

all by herself. Unfortunately or fortunately, depending on how I think about it, we grew up in foster homes and orphanages in the '50s. White kids were in the minority and race wasn't an issue. Nobody cared what color our skin was. What mattered most was what dormitory we lived in, what our locker number was, and what sports or musical instrument we played. Forty boys lived and slept in an open dormitory. Segregation – what's that?"

I had three prized possessions. (1) was my catcher's mitt, (2) was a coffee can full of marbles and (3) was a small transistor radio. Lots of kids back then had transistor radios, and the question was always "what should we listen to?" For me the answer was - Baseball!

I used to know every one of the players for the Chicago White Sox and the Chicago Cubs, as well as many of the players on the other teams as well. I knew their names, their positions, their jersey numbers, and I even knew many of their averages. Sometimes, I was lucky enough to have one of their baseball cards, but a pack of baseball cards with a piece of gum, back then, cost a nickel and nickels were hard to come by.

The boys in the orphanage would sometimes get to go to Wrigley Field, probably as a guest of the Chicago Cubs, due to our "circumstances." We would talk the bus driver into getting us there early, or into staying late, and if we were really lucky, we would get autographs or at least talk to one of the players.

I was never a good player, but I sure worshipped the men who played; they were my heroes!

After working my way up through the ranks of Jewel Foods, I left in the late '70s and franchised a couple of White Hen Family Convenient Stores. One of them was in Glendale Heights, a blue collar "white" suburb in DuPage County, west of Chicago.

In the mornings, the "guys" would congregate around the coffee pot, smoking cigarettes, eating donuts, drinking coffee, and discussing world events and sports.

Mr. Bill McCrary became a regular, and everybody liked him. All I knew about him, initially, was that he had been a welder for Electromotive, and was not working due to an injury.

He and his wife had relocated from Maywood, a predominately "Black" suburb after Mr. Bill went on disability. Once I found out that Mr. Bill had lived in Maywood, I told him that I had been the Assistant Jewel Food Store Manager in Maywood, back in the late '60s during the race riots, and it dawned on him he knew me way back then, as well. I don't remember if it was Mr. Bill or Mama Cleo who responded when I

43

asked, "Why did you move from Maywood to Glendale Heights?" The reply was "People should not live with people just like themselves; the world would be a better place if people who were different could figure out how to live together." I really liked that answer!

At the time, I had three beautiful daughters, all in elementary school, and I was trying to do everything I could to be a good parent. I had also come to the realization that the primary responsibility of a parent was to give their children the best education possible, give them the opportunity to make age appropriate decisions, and surround them with diversity.

The more time I spent with Mr. Bill, the more he became "the Father I wish I had". We would go fishing together, spend time with each other's families, and he and I played cards with the "guys" frequently.

One night, while playing cards one of the "guys" mentioned that he used to be a pitcher for the Chicago Cubs. His name around the card table was "Dicker," and when I asked what name he used when he played baseball, I remembered him. Once the discussion turned to baseball, Mr. Bill started talking about the days when he played baseball with the Kansas City Monarch's. He told us that he played with Jackie Robinson and Ernie Banks; to name just a few.

I had known these guys for a couple of years at this point, and now I discovered that they played baseball with my heroes when I was a kid growing up.

That was almost 40 years ago and Mr. Bill is, and has been, "the Dad I wished I had" for all those years. He and his wife welcomed and accepted me and my family into their lives, and we were very fortunate that they did so. Our lives together remind me of what it's like to read and live in a book. After finishing one chapter (if you're smart) you start reading and living the next chapter. With Mr. Bill and Mama Cleo, I realized there was always more to read and more to learn. They were willing to teach and I was an avid learner. Between the two of them, I learned lessons that helped me live a far better life than I ever imagined. I also learned lessons that helped me fulfill my dream of being a good parent, and I am confident that my daughter's benefited from the relationship and advice as well.

Mr. Bill was always pretty shy about talking about the "old days" early in our relationship. He was probably in his late 60s when Mama Cleo sat him down one day and told him that he played a very important part of American History, and that his story needed to be told. It's only been since that day that Mr. Bill has been willing and able to share with his family, friends and others, what it was really like. Because of all the time we spent together, I suspect he has shared more with me than he has with others.

Mama Cleo was absolutely correct, as she always was! Mr. Bill was a part of American History, and his story needed to be heard. My family and I have been very fortunate to be there with him and for him, as he has learned to share, enjoy and celebrate his past.

I have been honored and blessed to be Mr. Bill's "other" Son and have benefited more than I can he realizes. Thank you, Mr. Bill for being the Dad I wished I had. Segregation – What's that?

Pictured: Jake and family

Here's the pitch!

He's ready to release!

"Youngblood" waves to the crowd!

That February day, back in 2008, was a reminder that "no good deed goes unturned," and it made me know that I had done something right. I try to help anyone, in any way I can and this is proof that when you do good, good comes back to you. I have been blessed, and I thank God for so many good people in my life.

When someone does a good deed for Bill, he tries to hold onto something to remind him of that person. Jake doesn't seem to remember this letter or the contents it contained, but it's etched in the mind of the receiver, and he's forever grateful for Jake, the letter, and its contents.

A letter from Jake:

Jacob Fisher
856 Glades Court NE
St Petersburg, FL 33702

February 18, 2008

Dear Mama Cleo and Mr. Bill:

To be writing this letter to you gives me a tremendous amount of pride. As parents, you and I both know the amount of effort it takes to raise children and you and I both know that it takes more than just the Mother and the Father to have good outcomes.

The two of you have been very instrumental in helping me, raise, teach and influence my daughters. You've been there for me when I had questions or concerns. You've given me lots of advice and council, some of which I followed and obviously some of which I probably ignored. You've even given advice and council to my girls, some more than others and I couldn't be more proud of the outcome.

When I say I am a very proud parent, I say so knowing that I didn't do it alone and that your contributions were enormous.

I tell you all this because the contents of the envelope that is included with this letter came not just from me, but with a tremendous amount of pride, I can say that it came from all three of my daughters and my son-in-laws as well.

The girls are old enough now to understand that living on a fixed income isn't easy, especially when the cost of living keeps going up and just like me they want you to be able to enjoy your retirement years.

The two of you gave so much, when you had it to give and now it's time to be on the receiving end. Our gift isn't much, but more importantly, we want the both of you to know that we love you very much and when you need us we will be here for you.

With Love and gratitude,

Your "son" Jake
Amy, David, Aaron
Lorrie, Kevin, Jessica, Amanda
Deanna and Jay

Memories from Elaine McGraw Brannon, a young lady whom Bill trusts with everything, including his life:

I am a firm believer that God takes care of me, whether I can see physical evidence or not. Before I was born, my parents, Horace and Gladys McGraw, became friends with Bill and Cleo. They lived on the same street, but a block away from each other. Later, when my parents moved to the suburbs, Bill and Cleo purchased a home in the subdivision five minutes away. When Bill and Cleo retired, and moved to a retirement community, my parents purchased a home in the same community when they retired. When my mother was pregnant with me, Cleo promised her that if anything should happen to her and/or my father, that she and Bill would take the responsibility of raising me. I was born into that stability, and I didn't even know it.

As a toddler, my mother would walk me to the corner, so I could run across the street, into Cleo's arms, to spend the day with my other parents. While Cleo and I shared mother-daughter time talking, shopping, talking, running errands, talking, and eating ice cream (which we weren't supposed to tell Bill about all the time, but talking was my pastime, so I often spilled the beans), it was Bill who shared valuable lessons about how a man should love his wife. He talked often about what I should expect from boys and men from their grooming to their willingness to do

53

"man chores." Not because I didn't know how to do things (he knew my mother and father were raising me to be independent and a jack of all trades, like my father), but because that is another way a man expresses his love, he said. As he would vacuum the carpet (and tell me that I couldn't have any more sweets that day), he'd tell me how taking out the trash, washing the car and keeping it gassed, and going to work were all traits I would want in a man whether he was my friend, boyfriend, or husband. He was the only man I knew who could vacuum a carpet without leaving lines from the vacuum cleaner, so I hung on every word (my sister and I are still trying to master that skill). I often wondered how I'd end up with two coconut or windmill cookies (from his favorite cookie jar), when he said I couldn't have any more sweets for the day. To this day, when he's ready to drop knowledge, I find myself at that same cookie jar, and those same types of cookies are always there...Stability.

There were many cares of life for a girl born during the civil rights movement (1963), and growing up in a decade portrayed as a pivot of change. One thing that I was sure of was that if something tragic ever happened to my father, Bill would step in. What girl could ask for more with that kind of stability? As I entered college, preparing to embark on a career and independent living, I had the assurance of that stability.

When I went against my life plan, and accepted a marriage proposal, I had assurance of that stability. It was Bill who was second to my father in giving his paternal consent, and stamp of approval for my husband-to-be. They assured me that my husband would be their son. During our wedding ceremony, Bill and Cleo led our processional to the altar. He would not settle for wearing a nice suit, he had to have on a tuxedo and referred to himself as, "second father to the bride." Cleo purchased an official, "mother-of-the-bride" dress, and she orchestrated all the moving parts of the ceremony and both receptions for my mother, her girlfriend. Bill and Cleo blessed us with words of wisdom during our reception. Just years prior, at my brother's wedding, he stepped in as father-to-the-bride for my sister-in-law, when her father could not attend the wedding due to illness.

When I was diagnosed with breast cancer, at the age of 36, Bill and Cleo immediately got on the rotation as caregivers. They gave my parents and husband, a U.S. Navy Commander, relief, by staying with us during my entire radiation therapy. For nine weeks, five days a week, Bill drove me to the treatment center. He and Cleo took me to my first cancer survivor's event that summer, and encouraged me to walk the survivor's victory lap, which I didn't think I could complete. Coming around the track, it was as if I was winning an Olympic race because I could see him waving his arms frantically and screaming, "yea, go, go, go," because Cleo was crying too much to cheer. After treatment, I discussed with Cleo that I wanted every breast cancer survivor to feel the sense of celebration that they stirred in me at that event. When Troy and I developed our non-profit organization, Revivals Health & Wellness Council, and were presented with an opportunity to host a breast cancer survivor's luncheon, Cleo assured us that she and Bill would be major financial supporters. For the next eleven years, largely because of their generosity, breast cancer survivors in Northern Nevada have enjoyed a celebration like none other.

Though Cleo's passing away, three years ago, was a blow to me like none other, my relationship with Bill has not changed. We've been together over 50 years now. He does what fathers do: support, chastise, and direct. I do what daughters do: love, depend, support, and respect. I'm fulfilling the promise I made to Cleo many years ago, just like she promised my parents; that I would take care of Bill in the event that she could not (not too much Kool-Aid, an endless supply of ice cream, and cable TV, so he could watch all the baseball games televised). All in the name of the stability that binds us.

Pictured: Bill & Cleo

Bill & Cleo McCrary

Cleo McCrary, Elaine Brannon, Bill McCrary

Elaine McGraw Brannon is Founder and Director of Revivals Health & Wellness Council. She and her husband, Troy Brannon, U.S. Navy Commander (Ret), reside in Fernley, Nevada.

The Wedding Toast-Bill McCrary, Cleo McCrary, Troy Brannon, Elaine Brannon

Horace McGraw, Cleo McCrary, Gladys McGraw, Bill McCrary

Thoughts and Thankfulness by: Amy Thomason

My story of Bill McCrary is only 20 years old! But, I know it was no accident that Bill and his late wife, Cleo, bought a house up the street from my parents. We got to know each other at neighborhood get-togethers, and we became truly family. When they invited me to their church, Village Bible Church, Daddy and Bill were sports buddies, especially baseball. He loved Bill's stories!

Over the years, Bill and I shared moments when I knew he was a friend I could always count on! When the snowstorm of Christmas 2000 hit, Bill was one of the few people in the Village who had the know-how, and the right vehicle (still running), to help people out. Sure enough, he came to rescue me from no electricity, and made a second trip to rescue, Ranger, a cat he wasn't crazy about, named for a Baseball team he wasn't crazy about! In 2006, my Daddy died. I called Bill and Cleo, as I left the hospital, and, as I pulled in the driveway to my house, they were right behind me! Bill asked me to talk to him in the den - and proceeded to assure me that I had lost my daddy, but he would always be available to be a dad when I needed him. And he has! There's something very reassuring knowing that a dad is aware when you're late, or working too hard, and calls to check-in to make sure you're ok.

We've since then been through some fun times and some sad times. Cleo and my mother died one year apart, so we've filled in for their loss on holidays and special church times. And we make it a few times a year to Arkansas Traveler Games, in North Little Rock, where he loves to "backseat drive" when I score games; we love those debates!

Daddy taught me that Baseball was a game of strategy and teamwork. I believe Bill, especially, demonstrates teamwork in his life. There's no ego - just what can he do to help! And, Bill is also a man of faith. He unashamedly gives credit for his blessings to God. What more could you ask for? God has blessed me with a "second dad!"

Goddaughter Ida Cotton writes:

I met Bill and Cleo more than 30 years ago, when I started working for the United States Postal Service.

Since that time, Mr. Bill has been a constant in my life. We have traveled together, and I have spent many holidays at their home. Cleo became a mother figure to me when I lost my mom in 1994.

Then, I lost my dad in 2004, and Bill stepped in and filled a void that I couldn't imagine ever being filled. In my mind, they became my parents. I could not have loved them more if they were. I could always count on them for love, and sound advice in any situation. I can talk to

61

him about anything. I have enjoyed their presence in my life. I talk to Mr. Bill weekly by phone, and I try to visit as often as I can, but I am always there when he really needs me. I simply cannot imagine Mr. Bill not being a part of my life.

Loving memories from the Reverend Hadley Edwards: William McCrary "Mr. Bill" – A Tribute

I have known William McCrary most of my life. I consider him to be a family member. He is a man of deep faith, truth, and integrity. I met him when I was a young boy, working at the home of his Mother and Father-in-law, in Fulton, Missouri. Long before I knew anything about his journey with the Historic Negro Baseball League, he had already "hit the ball out of the park" for me. Mr. Bill shattered all the misconceptions of adverse relationships that is said to exist between a man and his Mother-in-law. Mr. Bill truly loved his Mother-in-law as his own Mother.

Mrs. Coates also shares the same feelings regarding him. I was impressed with the constant love and care he displayed for her until the close of her life.

Mr. Bill has always shown an interest in young people, and what they are doing in life and with their life.

Although I was the "Yard Boy," at the home of his in-laws, The Coates, he always took the time to inquire as to how I was progressing in school and in life. He took notice of the things I was doing, and he cared enough to share encouragement along the way. I accepted his advice and encouragement; as a young boy without a father figure in my life; as a solid stepping stone to a better and brighter future. He always knew the right things to say, and the manner in which to say it.

Our years of friendship and fellowship continue to this day. We have continued to stay in touch over the years.

As I write this tribute, I am reminded of the fact that Mr. Bill and his late wife, Cleatrice, gave me a trip to Chicago, as my high school graduation gift. I will never forget this because, as a poor boy from rural Missouri, it was an awesome gift, was and my first trip by airplane. I was able to experience the "big city" under their tourism expertise. They proved to be great historians, and knowledgeable about social studies, during that trip.

Just as we reflect on the history of the Old Negro League of Baseball, and remember its great moments, I reflect on the greatness of Mr. Bill: who is a role model, an inspiration to people everywhere, and a compassionate Christian Witness. Mr. Bill is in a league all by himself.

He represents a team of African-American men, who are growing smaller day-by-day. However, his influence will live forever because he continues to help so many as he passes through this life.

Mr. Bill, enjoy the honors and the applause you receive at this point in your life; for you have earned it by just being who you are, naturally. Wear that smile and garment of compassion forever, for there are many who will never be the same because you have touched their life.

Thank you for touching my life!

A Forever Friend and Fan,

Rev. Hadley R. Edwards

New Orleans District Superintendent of the United Methodist Church

New Orleans, Louisiana

Longtime friend, Dave Watson, remembers Bill:

"And then it happened!"

Cleo and Bill McCrary were out to dinner with friends at Hot Springs Village AR (their retirement home) as retirees do. The male usually controls the conversation with what accomplishments he had in life and in his career and, as it goes, the stories bounce back and forth as the evening progresses. Bill McCrary says nothing!

At the end of the evening Bill and Cleo are home. Bill could sense that Cleo had something on her mind and then it happened! Cleo turned to Bill and said "Come sit down. I have something to discuss with you". Bill sat in his chair and was ready to listen. If one had the opportunity to meet Cleo, one would know that she was a no nonsense lady. Cleo then proceeded to tell Bill that they listen to all these stories of their friends and the life experiences that they have had. Bill sits there and says nothing. Cleo went on to say that Bill had an outstanding career in baseball and this was a story that needed to be told. If Bill wasn't going to tell the story, Cleo was!

"And then it happened!"

Bill and I first met in the work place at Electro Motive Div. of GM. He was a welder and I was an electrician. We grew close working together day in and day out. As both careers started to progress and we stepped into management positions, our friendship continued to grow. As the years passed, we would get together socially. We became BEST OF FRIENDS. I hope this book provides an overview of Bill's career and tells the story of what trials and tribulations he went through.

It was once written and I keep referring back to this quote as I grow older, "A real friend makes you think the best thoughts about yourself." Bill was that friend!

Dave Watson
GM Business Manager (retired

When questioned about school sports, Bill answered, "I really didn't play any sport in school, but basketball. I excelled in all sports though. They came very easy for me. Baseball wasn't played in school. It was an after-school sport, and I played on several teams."

When asked about his love for the game of baseball, Bill said, "For as long as I can remember, I played baseball and loved the game." It was at Lincoln Jr. high school that he became the first, and only (that he knows of), to achieve the largest "L" (tennis, basketball, track, wrestling, and of course baseball). To this day, he doesn't know if anyone else at the school ever achieved a larger "L."

"I played with the little league and several other teams throughout my junior high and high school years, and I played with some fantastic guys from those teams."

Pictured: Bill enjoying a banquet

Bill as a child (right front; inside)

Pictured: The Janesville Cubs

Bill (left; front) kneels with his baseball team, the Janesville Cubs.

Birds Place Two Players On Star '9'

The Beloit Red Birds placed two players on the Southern division's all-star squad for the Central league's summer classic late this month at Wilmot.

Bill McCreary, veteran handyman, was named to the third base assignment while Tom Mallett will serve as an alternate first baseman with Milton's Irwin Dade.

Catch Billy Hill, outfielder Larry Pohlman and shortstop Jack Freeman missed berths by a single vote.

Others named to the squad were Milton catcher Bill Liske, Milton second baseman Larry Landenheim, Whitewater shortstop Ken Beaick, Elkhorn's Ron Smith as an alternate infielder and outfielders Don Timmer of Wilmot, Ralph Mardinger of Whitewater, Al Lehman of Walworth and Bob Kuckenbecker of Janesville.

The Southern pitchers will be Whitewater's Bill Fardy, Sharon's George Hertel, Wilmot's Norm Benedict and ...

The Beloit Red Birds

Pictured: Sharon, Wisconsin newspaper clipping

Pictured: newspaper clippings featuring Bill and teammates

Top: Bill (second row; center right) Middle: Bill, kicking up dust as a shortstop

An article posted in the Beloit Daily News on September 26, 2013, written by Jim Franz, conveys a message and speaks tons, as to whether Bill McCrary was big league material.

Beloit's baseball had been segregated since the 1920s. For decades, the all-Black Beloit Red Sox, Tigers, and Phillies played their games at Edgewater Park. White teams played across town, at Summit Park.

When the Daily News published a story in 1997, about sandlot baseball at Edgewater Park, McCrary's name was front and center.

"He played third, short, he could run, hit and throw," Carl Edwards, of the 1940s Phillies, said. "I think everyone agrees: he was the best."

Lawrence Hoskins, another ex-Phillie, said, "McCrary was amazing. Of all the guys I played with, he was the one I thought could have been a big league player.

"Even in the 1950s, it was hard for a Black guy to make it to the majors. If you weren't a sure-fire star, you usually were let go."

Bill McCreary Signs with Janesville '9'

Janesville—Bill "Bootch" Mc-Creary, Beloit Red Birds third baseman during the past three months, has signed a Janesville Cub contract, business manager Sherman Hall announced today. He will start at third base when the Cubs meet Green Bay there tonight.

Standing 5' 9½" and weighing 160 pounds, McCreary is the second player from Beloit to sign with the State league class D club within the past month. Gary Wolfe, hurler for the Junior Legion nine during 1949-50, inked a Janesville pact about three weeks ago.

The 0-year old Negro has been

"When I signed with Janesville Cubs, I was only about twenty miles from home, but the harsh treatment was ever present. You would think being right around the corner from home would make it better, but it didn't. Janesville Cubs was a Yankee team for Chicago Cubs."

Bill (3rd from left); Ray Whitlow (4th from left)

Going over some of the articles, Bill points out, that not only did many get it wrong about the Negro Baseball League being a semipro or minor league at that time, but players "names were often misspelled, and their stats and info lost or they were inaccurate.

"When I played for the Redbirds team, a guy named Ray Whitlow was there. He was a real good friend. We called ourselves the 'best double play combination ever.' I went to Taylorville, Illinois looking for Ray once because I knew that was his hometown. Nobody I talked with seemed to know him, so I never saw him again. I was informed later that he had died in 2009."

Chapter 4: Trying Out for Pro Baseball

It was Bill's senior year, when the pressures of playing the game became a driving force. Guidance came from others, such as Harry Pohlman (American Legion coach) who approached him about leaving school to go tryout for the league, but Bill knew his father would not approve of that. His father would insist that he finish school ahead of playing ball.

The St. Louis Cardinals' scouts came to town recruiting. He remembers riding his bike to the tryouts for big league baseball, at the insistence of Coach Pohlman, but there were lots of guys there being separated into groups, and who were told to come to the center of the field. When he saw this, Bill got on his bike and rode home. "I just knew they wouldn't take me. For one thing, I was young, and I didn't think they were serious about us trying out. The place was filled with white players, so I figured the whites would be picked anyway. I was the only Black."

That evening, coach Pohlman and the talent scout knocked on his door, and wanted to talk to Mr. McCrary about letting Bill tryout for the league. He played one season with the league in 1946, but had to return home because his dad insisted he finish high school before any ball playing.

"He was a stickler about getting my education."

Bill said, "I'm grateful to Mr. Pohlman, who is the main reason for my journey to the Negro Baseball League. He was relentless in pushing me because he knew I had potential, and he believed in me. I knew I wouldn't get a chance for St. Louis, but Mr. Pohlman promised to put me with the best team in the Negro League."

He returned to Kansas City in 1947 under the supervision of Satchel Paige. Satchel called a meeting of the players after I arrived and said, "Now we got some young blood."

"My nickname 'Youngblood' was born," said Bill with pride. "From then on I was known as Youngblood and Satchel Paige gave it to me."

Satchel took me under his wings, and took care of me like a father would've. He made sure I ate, slept and was taken care of all around. When we went on trips, he made sure I had everything I needed because he had promised my dad that he would look after me. He also made sure I didn't hear any negative stuff that surrounded the league because he did not want me to be discouraged. I did find out later.

When asked about any other nicknames he had, he quietly said, "I was known as *Bootch* McCrary in Beloit, but I really don't know where that one came from. The new one took hold, and pretty soon everyone was referring to me as *Youngblood*. I liked that one better."

I was there when Branch Rickey came for Jackie Robinson. He didn't go straight to the Dodgers. He went somewhere in Canada first.

Now, Jackie was not the best in the league. There were guys, like Josh Gibson and Satchel Paige, who were much better ball players than Jackie, and they were kind of upset because they thought they should've had the first opportunity. Branch knew what he was doing by picking Jackie first because many of the men in the league would not have put up with what he endured.

Jackie was an educated man, who had been in the armed services and went to Officers' School. In fact, there were some who quit after making it to the majors because they couldn't take all the harsh treatment.

We had it bad. I mean really bad.

Chapter 5: Kansas City Monarchs

Finally, after making it back to the Kansas City Monarchs, life was at its highest for Bill. Ernie Banks moved to another team, and eventually onto the majors, which paved the way for Bill to replace Ernie as shortstop, but Ernie didn't go directly to the majors. First, he went to a Yankee Farm team.

"I was only seventeen in a man's world, but I'd played baseball all my life; often the only Black on the team. I was in the real world; now playing with real heavyweights, but I really didn't pay any attention to that. We were just ballplayers."

Thinking about all the good times, Bill laughed, and shook his head saying, "Satchel was a pool shark too; meaning, he played for money. I think everything he did revolved around how to make money. He would take me with him in the evenings, when he went to shoot pool. I learned the game from him, and he was good, one of the best."

Pictured: An article photographed from the Beloit Daily News

THE BELOIT (WIS.) DAILY NEWS, TUESDAY AU...

McCrary Gets Chance with KC Monarchs

One of the happiest boys in Beloit last night was Billy McCrary, or as he is known to most of his Junior Legion circles, it's Billy Page. Tom Baird, owner of the Kansas City Monarchs, telephoned Bill and his Coach H. C. Pohlman last evening and made arrangements for the little Legion age to report...

B. McCrary ... Kansas City Friday where the Monarchs are playing a weekend engagement.

Baird would like to have McCrary report to Council Bluffs, Ia., tomorrow night where the Monarchs play, and then travel with the club to St. Joseph, Mo., enroute. Traveling and expenses could not be arranged quick enough for that, so Billy is reported to Street Hotel in Kansas City. Baird said that he expect... ...him eight to 10 days...

Kruegers
Lockwood 1b
Belardi 2b
Vapraskas 3b
Gunderson lf
Wegner p
Partridge c
Sumpter cf
Gupton cf
Wilson rf
Webster rf
Totals
Crowleys
Smith c
Pipitone rf
Naidenovich lf
Crowley 1b
Pellegrini 3b
Sreenan cf

79

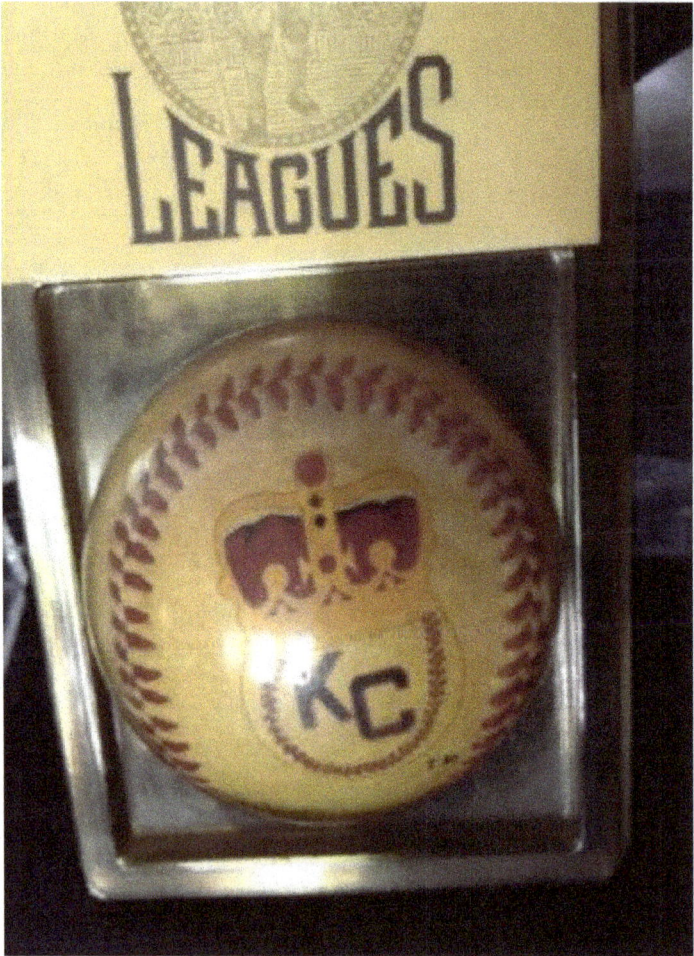

While playing for the Kansas City Monarchs, Bill found himself playing against or alongside baseball greats, such as Satchel Paige, Buck O'Neil, Ernie Banks and many others. He was there when Jackie Robinson joined the team. When Jackie got to Kansas City, he stayed to himself a lot. There was no doubting how he felt about the overall mindset of people about the Negro League and Black baseball, and he wanted no part of it.

"Many people ask me about Josh Gibson, but I didn't play with Josh. I knew him, but I never played with him. Now, I played with and for Satchel and Buck. I never played with "Cool Papa Bell," but I knew him because he came to the baseball reunions," Bill said.

Many of the guys weren't happy that Jackie was picked to break the barrier into Major League baseball. They knew he wasn't the best player in the league, but Bill says, "Looking back, Branch Ricky made a good decision to push Jackie because he was educated; he knew how to handle himself in any situation, and most of the players wouldn't have taken all the cruel treatment Jackie endured. Jackie was an officer, and learned discipline in the armed forces and it showed.

"Buck O'Neil had a different opinion. He thought Satchel would've been a better choice, and could've handled the situation a lot better than Jackie did, and people would have seen Satchel as the superstar he was; the icon that people loved. He said they only looked at Jackie as a symbol; just a Black man."

Satchel was getting up in age at that time, but he was still on his game, and he and others thought they should've gone before Jackie. One player, Hilton Smith, left the league, went to Mexico, and never came back. A few others did exactly the same. The harsh treatment was more than they could stand.

The Monarchs (owned by white businessman, J.L. Wilkinson), were one of the best known and most successful Black teams. Tying the Homestead Grays for the most flags by any Negro League team, the Monarchs captured a total of ten pennants, and suffered only one losing season during their entire association with the Negro Leagues. That season was during World War II because the roster was devastated by the loss of players to the military. The Monarchs also hold the distinction of having won the first World Series ever played between opposing leagues, both in the initial World Series in 1924 (between the Negro National League and the Eastern Colored League), and again in the reinstated World Series in 1942 (between the Negro National League and the Negro American League).

The Monarchs, a charter member of the Negro National League, played through the 1930 season, winning pennants in 1923-1925 and in 1929. The team never experienced a losing season. They narrowly missed a fourth straight pennant in 1926, when they won the first half title, but lost a bitter nine game playoff to the Chicago American Giants after dropping a doubleheader on the last day. Facing the Hillsdale team on both occasions, the Monarchs played in the first two World Series ever played.

After dropping out of the league, The Monarchs played independent ball, until joining the Negro American League, as a charter member in 1937. The team remained a member, even after the league lost its major status. During the first six seasons (1937-1942), they won five pennants, except in 1938. After the return of some of their best players, who had been called to service during World War II, they annexed another flag in 1946. In 1942, the first World Series since 1927 was played between the Monarchs and the Homestead Grays, with the Monarchs sweeping the Grays in four straight games. In 1946, the Monarchs lost a tough seven game Series to the Newark Eagles. When the Monarchs won the second half of the split season, but lost a seven game playoff with the Birmingham Black Barons in 1948, they missed a chance to appear in the last Negro World Series ever played. The Negro National League folded, following that World Series, and the Negro American League took over some of the franchises, and expanded into division play. The Monarchs won the first half title in 1949, and annexed a division title in 1950.

Tom Baird continued to operate the Monarchs through the 1950s, after the franchise was sold to him by Wilkinson (following the 1948 season), but by then the league was strictly a minor league operation.

Bill reiterates, "I don't regret a thing because it was one of the most memorable and happiest moments in my life, when I arrived in Kansas City to join The Kansas City Monarchs. I wanted to play major league baseball, but the times were different. I knew I could've made it, but at that time there were only sixteen teams in the majors, and there were lots of very good players competing, so I knew it would be difficult. Still I have no regrets."

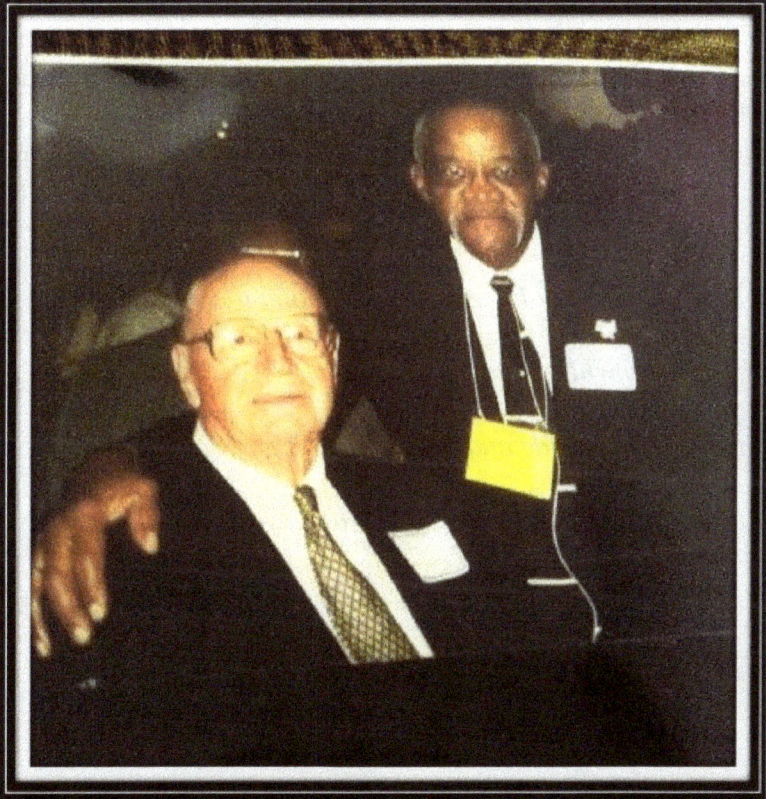

Bill with J.L. Wilkinson, owner of the Kansas City Monarchs

Chapter 6: Meandering Down Memory Lane

After leaving the Kansas City Monarchs, Bill embarked on a new venture with the Fargo Morehead Twins in Fargo, North Dakota, and gained a very good friend named Tracy, whom he named his son for.

This guy was an angel in disguise, and a very good friend. He took me under his wings, and treated me like a brother when we were playing together. When I went down there to play ball, I couldn't stay in the individual home where everyone else stayed. They didn't want me because I was Black, and when I was taken to a hotel for a room. Tracy made my stay there worthwhile because he'd come every day to pick me up. He'd say, "Let's go for a ride and grab something to eat." This was every day, and I really appreciated that. I was a long way from home where nobody wanted me, but Tracy was a gem. I can't remember his last name, but I really wish I could see him again.

I remember once, while playing for The Fargo Morehead Twins, under Mr. Tolleson, we went to spring training in either Oklahoma or Missouri or somewhere. I don't remember exactly where, but I walked to the front desk of the hotel, where the team was staying, and told the gentleman my name, and said I had a room there in the hotel. He looked at me and said no, you don't have a room in this hotel. I asked him to call

Mr. Tolleson, and told him what the man told me. He came down and told the clerk if I couldn't stay there he needed to call all the rooms that had players and tell them to come on down because we're leaving. Well, he changed his tune, and I was given a room.

It was way back in a corner somewhere, but I had a room. Then, we all went to eat and they wouldn't serve me. They told Mr. Tolleson that I couldn't eat there. Mr. Tolleson told them if I couldn't eat, nobody was eating, and we're leaving. They let me eat! Afterwards, anytime someone gave us a hard time about me being there, Mr. Tolleson gave me the money to pay the bill.

The Fargo Morehead Twins wasn't the only team Bill played with. There were a few others: The Chicago Cubs' farm teams, the Yankee's farm teams, and the Omaha Rockets.

Pictured: Bill reporting to the Janesville Cubs

When asked about the most memorable men of baseball from his time and from his standpoint, Bill replied, "There were so many great players I can't name them all."

Quoted from the book, *When the Game was Black and White*, Satchel Paige said, "I liked playing against Negro League teams, but I loved barnstorming. It gave us a chance to play everybody and go everywhere and let millions of people see what we could do. I just loved it. I'd have played every day of the year if I could."

I had great respect for Satchel Paige because he took care of me when I left home. Remember, I was just a young boy, fresh out of high school, and I'd never been away from my family. Every morning, he would come get me for breakfast. He made sure I ate, and didn't get too homesick. He was my mentor, and father away from home. We kept busy. I remember when we were barnstorming (traveling from place-to-place) with The Satchel Paige All-Stars. Satchel was flying in, and it was getting late (time wasn't a factor for Satchel). Sometimes, he didn't even show up for games, if he got a better offer for another. He arrived at the last minute, warmed up with three pitches, and said, "I'm ready to play."

I didn't know any pitcher who could warm up with three pitches, and be ready for a game. Satchel was extraordinary, to say the least. He went out there and pitched seven innings of no hits; no runs baseball. The seventh inning, he called us all in, except the catcher and said, "Sit down." We thought he had lost his mind; nobody on the field, but him and the catcher! He struck out the side and waved at the crowd. He knew what he was doing. This game was with the West League All-Stars, and Ernie Banks was on that team. Satchel brought people out to see us. He was a drawing card. He knew how to make money, and he made it. I'd say he was a negotiator, and he could do that because everybody wanted him. His skills were unmatched. Satchel did things no one else could do.

That's why he was always busy. He'd leave one game, and be right on another field. That's also why he often made it to a game right at the nick of time. Satchel had a hesitation pitch that they wouldn't let him use in the majors. I tell you he was something else, and in 1971, he was the first Black man to be named to the hall of fame for his career in the Negro Baseball League alone.

Buck O'Neil, I can't say enough good things about this man. I credit him with reuniting the players, and keeping the Negro League in the forefront. I absolutely admired this man. He was a great ball player, mentor, and leader. I played with him, and for him, at the Monarchs. Although it came a little late for some of the guys, he started our reunions and kept us in focus. In my book, he was bigger than life. I looked up to him, as the father of the Negro Baseball Reunions Founder and Innovator, and I'll forever be grateful to him for reuniting us, and making sure we weren't a forgotten league.

Everything this man did, he did for a reason. He was awesome, and conscientious. You know Buck was still driving his car when he was ninety four years old?

I remember once going to Kansas City to visit the baseball museum and a friend of mine, James Davis, asked me to bring him a signed baseball of Buck O'Neil; if I happen to see him. I told him that I would. He instructed me that he didn't want anyone's signature on the ball, but Buck's. Well, I was able to get it, and I brought it back to him, but I didn't get one for myself. When Buck passed away, my friend gave the ball back to me, and told me that I needed that ball.

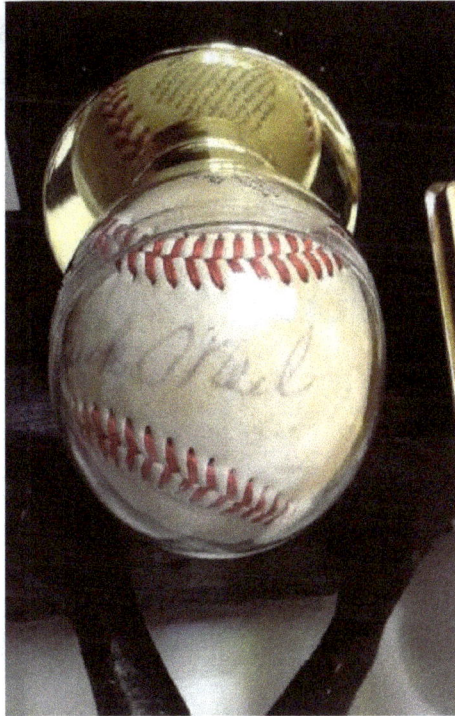

Bill, Cleo and Buck

Then there's "Cool Papa" Bell. He was quite a religious man, and didn't like to be around any swearing or bad talking. He was fast as lightning.

I have to tell you the story of the time he and Satchel (as Satchel told it to me) were traveling with the B team of the Monarchs, called the Little Monarchs or Traveling Monarchs, when Cool Papa made Satchel a bet he could turn the light off, and be in bed before it actually goes out. They had a discussion on the way to the room about Cool Papa being the fastest man ever, and Satchel told him he was getting old and wasn't as fast as he used to be. Cool Papa had already made the assessment earlier that the light was delayed in coming on when the switch was turned off, so he challenged Satchel after a waning argument. Satchel fell all in, and it ended up costing him a "cool" fifty dollars to find out that one human being was faster than the speed of light, "Cool Papa" Bell. Maybe, Satchel should've known better, but he fell for it nevertheless.

Another one of the many stories, about the faster-than-a-bullet Bell, is the time he caught up with his own ball. He was hit by it while rounding first base, and was called out. Now that's faster than the speed of light and sound!

Ted "Double Duty" Radcliffe is another who was a memorable figure to me. He was dynamic also. They called him "Double Duty" because he used to pitch the first game of a double header, and played catcher in the second one. "Double Duty" was 103-years-old, when he died in 2005.

He also had a way with the gals. Always pulling double duty, he didn't care whether they were young or old, as long as they wore a dress.

Even in his wheelchair, he was a schmoozer because he loved women. He was quite the ladies' man!

Pictured: Ted "Double Duty" Radcliffe, Unknown, and Buck O'Neil at a Reunion.

More cards

Pictured: Bill and Mamie Johnson (One of the three women who played baseball in the Negro Baseball League).

Pictured: A baseball hat signed by many great players, including: Charley Pride (the country western singer and Negro League Baseball Player), and his brother, Mack.

Pictured: More signatures on the hat.

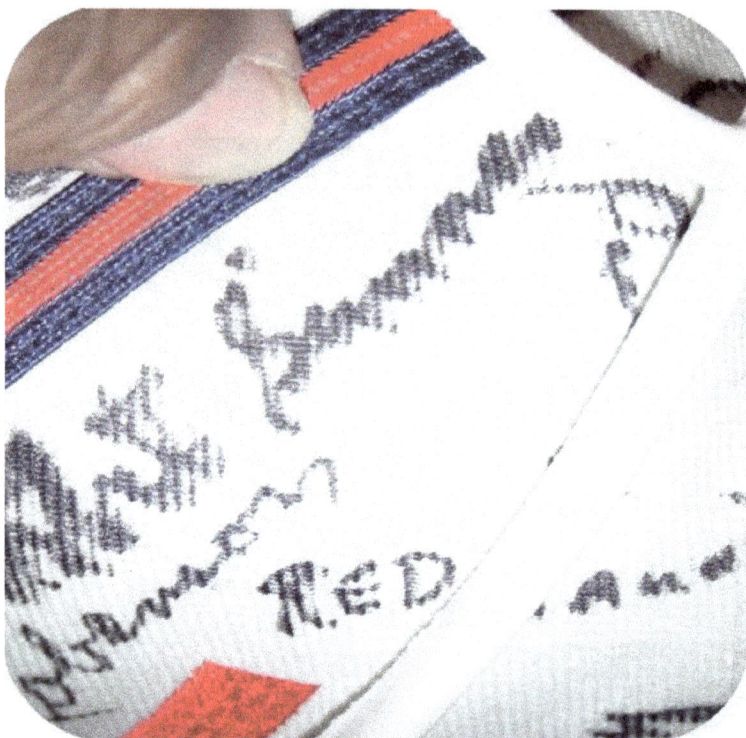

Pictured below: Signature of Charley Pride's brother, Mack

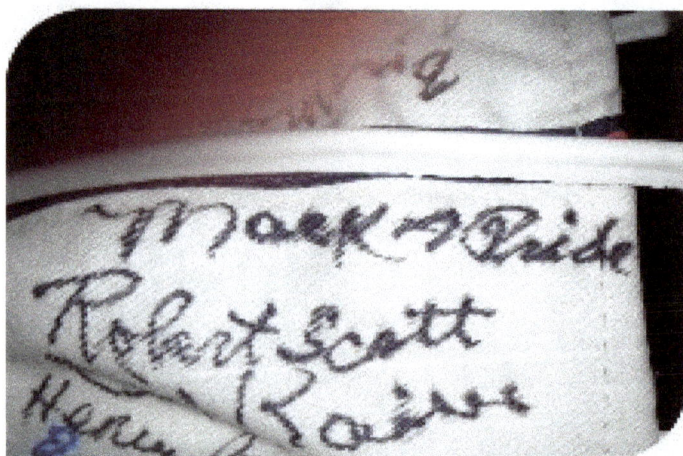

I remember once traveling with the Satchel Paige Traveling Monarchs to Oklahoma, to play an exhibition game. We stopped right on the outskirts because we knew we wouldn't be able to get rooms, nor eat in the town. We were going to sleep on the bus, as we had many, many times before. The local police circled our bus about every hour to make sure everything was on.

The next morning, the blaring of music awakened us. It was a band from town that had come to escort us in. There had been a tornado that went through the night before, and tore up the white section of town. In the Black section, the sun was shining, people were going about business as usual, and even had clothes hanging on the clotheslines. They welcomed us in with open arms, and told us if we come back again to come on into town, and they would provide places to sleep and eat. This group of people included all the ethnic groups in the town.

I tried to go to as many reunions as I could because this was the only way we kept in touch. I was so impressed with being in the same room with, and meeting, Johnny Bench that I asked for his autograph. He turned to me and said that he wanted my autograph. This made me feel like I was ten feet tall. After all the years I had played, and felt so *irrelevant, to get asked for my autograph by Johnny Bench, I was floored!*

I've always admired this man, and I got an autograph just the way I liked.

I used to get fan letters all the time, but lots of them I read and threw away. I wish I had kept them now, along with all the other memorabilia I discarded. I just didn't think it was that important. This is a fan letter I received, all the way from Japan. This really impressed me

Fan letter from Japan:

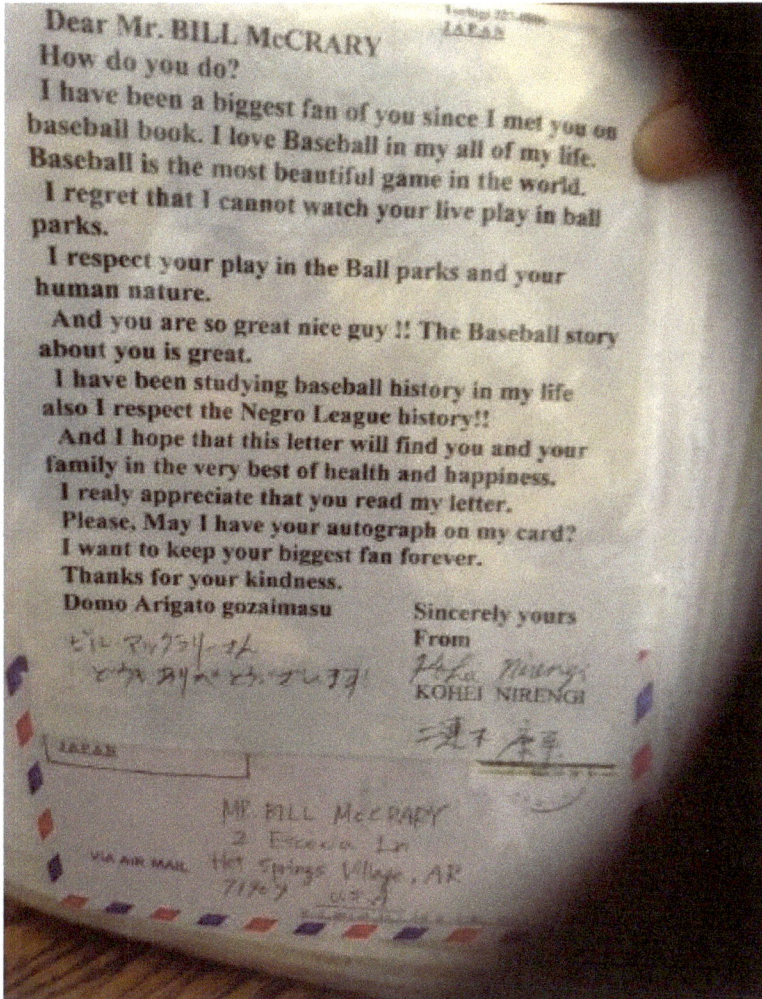

Dear Mr. BILL McCRARY

How do you do?

I have been a biggest fan of you since I met you on baseball book. I love Baseball in my all of my life. Baseball is the most beautiful game in the world.

I regret that I cannot watch your live play in ball parks.

I respect your play in the Ball parks and your human nature.

And you are so great nice guy !! The Baseball story about you is great.

I have been studying baseball history in my life also I respect the Negro League history!!

And I hope that this letter will find you and your family in the very best of health and happiness.

I realy appreciate that you read my letter.

Please, May I have your autograph on my card?

I want to keep your biggest fan forever.

Thanks for your kindness.

Domo Arigato gozaimasu

Sincerely yours
From
KOHEI NIRENGI

MR. BILL McCRARY
2 Escoda Ln
Hot Springs Village, AR
71909

The following pictures are from some of the baseball reunions Bill attended. He enjoyed connecting with people who shared his interests, as well as meeting new faces from the league.

the Following are in Attendance Tonight

George Altman	Jesse Askew	Bill Bell
Jim Carter	Charlie Davis	Ross Davis
Willie Harris	John W. Head	Carl Holden
Herman "Doc" Horn	Cowan Hyde	Clarence Jenkins
Ulysses Holliman	Connie Johnson	Ernest Johnson
Robert Landers	Carl Long	Joseph Marbury
Rendon Marbury	Jim "Lefty" La Marque	Rev. Henry Mason
William McCrary	Lee Moody	Bob Motley
John "Buck" O'Neil	Merrell Porter	Henry Presswood
Ted Rasberry	Jesse Rogers	Robert Scott
Eugene Scruggs	Alvin Spearman	A. "Slick" Surratt
Thomas Turner	Bill Van Buren	Larry Williams

Widows In Attendance

Mrs. Henry Bayliss	Mrs. Dewitt "Woody" Smallwood
Mrs. Hilton Smith	Mrs. Jesse Williams

1995 Player Reunion.
Photo courtesy of John Wakefield.

104

Bill is shown here with: **Charlie Davis-Memphis Reds** (top left); **Carl Long-Birmingham Black Barons** (top right); **Henry Presswood – KC Monarchs and Cleveland Buckeyes** (center left); **Ted Rasberry – KC Monarchs** (center right); **Ray Maupin – Bat boy KC Monarchs** (bottom left); and **Joseph Marbury – Indianapolis Indians** (bottom right)

Bill poses for a photo with his godson, Jake, and the legendary Buck O'Neil.

Bill's goddaughter Ida enjoys a moment with the legendary Double Duty below, while Bill (right) smiles for the camera

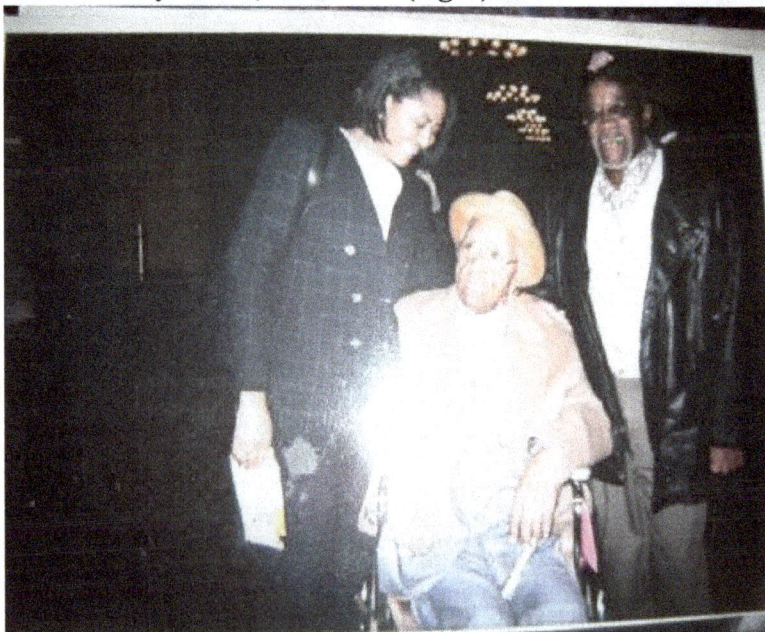

Pictured: Buck O'Neil and Bill McCrary 1997

Chapter 7: Life After Baseball

Bill held jobs at Alcoa and General Motors Corporation; putting in twelve years for each company, before becoming an entrepreneur with a janitorial cleaning service for eight years. He also coached and umpired little league baseball for five years.

Those jobs were rewarding, but they were just jobs. I had to work because I had a family to take care of.

When I started my own floor cleaning business for tile floors, it was the most gratifying for me because I made pretty good money in it, until two businessmen starting stealing my customers. They would go to my customers, and underbid me for the jobs. One day, they approached me about buying the business. I told them my price, and at first they didn't have the money, but eventually they paid after they realized I wasn't going to budge from my price.

Bill said, "One of my most rewarding jobs was related to baseball. It was a job coaching little league for five years. It gave me joy to see those young people put their best foot forward, literally, because they loved the game."

Pictured: Bill's little league team

Bill never talked to many people about what he did, and when he did it was very nonchalantly. When asked about his jobs, and the kind of work he did, Bill always referred to Alcoa Aluminum, General Motors, and the business he started up later. He never considered that the years he played baseball with the Negro League a job.

"I just never thought of playing ball as a job, even though I was paid for it. I regarded it as pure passion."

When asked about the pay he received playing baseball, he stated, "I made more money playing for the Yankee Farm teams than I made playing in the Negro League. That's why you found many players, especially Blacks, who left the country to play. They made loads of cash in places like Mexico, Venezuela, and the Dominican Republic, and even Colombia."

When asked about the most memorable personal event of his baseball career, Bill responded, "I was playing semi pro with the Beloit Redbirds in Knowlton, Wisconsin. My ex-wife, son, and her mother and father were with me. I was the only Black on the team, and every time I would go up to bat, a heckler in the stands would call me names. We had gotten to a critical point in the game, at the seventh inning, when I went up to bat, and we were behind 1-0 and had two men on base. It was hard to concentrate with the name calling, so I called "time out," and walked to the fence. I couldn't get to him because the fence was about 20 feet high, but I yelled to him, and I asked him if he would just refrain from the name calling, and let me concentrate, as I was trying to help my team have a chance to win. The crowd booed him out of the stands. I went back up to bat, and pulled the team up. We went on to win 2-1."

Bill always said he excelled in *any* sport, and bowling was no exception. It became a favorite pastime for Bill and Cleo. They joined and traveled with a local league, and many times he came out the winner; smelling like a rose.

Pictured: Bill's bowling league in Maywood, Illinois

Bill and Cleo (top photo; centered) enjoyed playing with their bowling league. In the bottom photo, Bill is seen kneeling in front of his teammates, after winning a championship.

Pictured: Bill and Cleo in local newspaper; honored for their achievements in bowling.

PRIZE WINNERS

MAYWOOD DO'

The rematch
Wisconsin, an
place last Sunda
arena. The eve
of two matches
cities. Maywoo
match when th
won their game
ies. The wome
less fortunate
with three wins
The event last
wood victorious
and series for
won by Velma
game and ser
was won by Bill
After the ga
enjoyed an even
at the home o
Simmons Dona
Avenue.

Velma Burnette and Bill McClary pose for pictures after winning high game and series in the match with Beloit last Sunday. Velma was high with a 179 game scratch and 598 series with handicap. Bill McClary was high with a 240 game with handicap and a 640 series with handicap.

Chapter 8: Retirement

Sitting around doing nothing was the farthest thing from Bill's mind. One day Cleo told him that he should retire, so they could travel some. That thought had never entered his mind, but two weeks later he came home, and he announced that he had retired. This is when he sold his floor cleaning business. He and Cleo traveled a lot after retirement. They both loved going places; seeing new things.

He remembers a time they were headed to Cancun, Mexico. He knew the McGraw's were going, but Cleo didn't. They were walking down the aisle at the airport, heading straight toward the McGraw's, and Cleo looked at him and said, "There's the McGraw's. I wonder where they're going."

When we met, they asked us if we were going to Cancun. We told them "yes," and Cleo couldn't stop laughing. She was so happy. The McGraw's and I had prearranged it, but she didn't figure it out until later.

The most memorable vacations of all (his response when asked about favorite vacations) were the times he spent in Fulton, Missouri with Cleo's mother.

Bill with Cleo's mother Susie

"I got along very well with her. As a matter of fact, she was one of the best women I've ever known. I loved her so much. I remember driving all the way to Fulton on the Wednesday before Thanksgiving, having dinner with her mother, then driving all the way back to Chicago in time for work the next day.

I loved her, as a son loves his mother. In fact, I once told her, if anything were to happen to her daughter (I didn't know what she would do if something happened to me), I'm coming home. That's how much I loved being with her. She also had an uncle that I loved dearly."

AUG • 63

Bill with Cleo's uncle Buck

Chapter 9: Moving to Hot Springs Village, Arkansas

I always thought about moving to a warmer climate, but I had no idea I'd end up in Arkansas. I had never even heard of Hot Springs Village, until a realtor mentioned it, and said this is a place we should check-out for retirement.

She set it up, for us to visit, and contacted a realtor there. Cleo said, "Let's at least go, and have a look at the place. We may like it."

I said, "Arkansas?"

I had my sights set on Fulton, where my mother-in-law lived. I tell you; I loved that woman. She was a good, good person.

Cleo never wanted to move back to her hometown. She wanted to explore, and possibly find a new interesting place to live. We flew into Arkansas, and settled in our condo, and then the realtor came to show us around. When we had looked around some, and eventually came to Calella, I told him that he didn't have to show me anything else. He asked me why. I told him because I like what I've seen so far, but he insisted on showing me more.

When we got back on the plane heading home, Cleo asked what I planned to do. I told her we would go back, and put our house on the market. That house sold in two weeks, a lot sooner than we had

117

anticipated, and they wanted us out right away. We were able to compromise, and we made our move in 1993 or 1994.

We came to Arkansas for a visit, but we fell in love with the place. I'm sure glad I listened to our realtor because I love it here. We've made some super friends, and Cleo (I called her Sweetie) and I have been very happy here. It's been twenty years now, and I wouldn't want to live anyplace else.

Pictured top and bottom: Oaklawn Racetrack 2000 and 2001; Hot Springs, Arkansas

Top: Bill (2nd row; 4th from right) Bottom: Bill (2nd left)

Chapter 10: Life Changing Events

It should have been an ordinary, but it was an extraordinarily sad day, when in 2011, Cleo (who had unusually small veins, which made it hard to draw blood when needed) was admitted into the hospital to have a port inserted for easy blood draw. It was an uncomplicated procedure, and only took a short time to complete. She had other medical problems, including a bad heart.

"My assistant pastor accompanied me to the hospital that morning. Cleo had a few medical problems, including heart troubles. We laughed and talked. She made us go have breakfast, and then some lunch, before the procedure was to begin. The doctor gave us a time; about twenty minutes, and then it would be over. The time came and went. Soon, the doctor came out, and I noticed the look on his face."

"She didn't make it."

"What did you say?"

"She's gone. She had a heart attack. We tried to revive her, but it did no good. I'm sorry."

That day, Bill's life changed forever. They were married for 52 years and now his "Sweetie" was gone. He said, "I just couldn't believe it. She was so happy that morning that something was going to finally be done, so she didn't have to go through the agony of all those needle sticks before hitting the right spot."

"I never imagined a life without Cleo, and it's still hard, especially around the holidays. I try to go on, as normal as I can, but it takes its toll at times," he said, with tears in his eyes.

His son Tracy was there to support him through it all, giving him a shoulder to lean on, and he is thankful for his son every day. Everything has a time, a season, and a reason. Bill, and those who know him best, agree God chose, in His perfect will, to heal the relationship that was distant, to mend two hearts that had been torn apart, and to reunite a bond that should never have been broken.

I volunteered several places, and one was in the outpatient area of the St. Joseph Hospital in Hot Springs, before my vision started failing, but I never went into the outpatient area where she died. I just couldn't bring myself do that one.

Nowadays, I find peace in just watching sports on television. I'll watch any sport because I love any of them, but my heart is still with baseball. I have always found satisfaction and solace in helping others and reading my bible. I read scriptures every morning. Now that my eyesight is failing, the blessings are returning to me. People are helping me, and they don't mind because I have helped others and always try to be good to everyone.

Cleo did an amazing thing for Bill, before her untimely passing. When they were visiting the Negro League Museum in Kansas City, she grabbed him by the arm, and led him to a display. He referenced what she said, "Bill, come here. Let me show you something.' It was a picture of me. She said, 'It's time you realize that you are a part of history, and that you need to tell your story. If you don't, I will."

Until then, he never really gave it much thought, but he suddenly realized that she was exactly right. So, he started talking, and hasn't quit.

Bill and Cleo

Chapter 11: The "Shades of Greatness" Event

The Negro League Baseball Museum has made great strides to make certain these men of baseball will never be forgotten. The museum, located in Kansas City, MO, contains a wealth of information, pictures, art, and memorabilia.

The *Shades of Greatness* is a traveling exhibit that was started by the museum in 2004. It displays a telling history of the baseball league, and some of the players who were dedicated to the game, and contributed so much to it.

In August 2013, the exhibit opened in Little Rock, Arkansas at the Mosaic Templars Cultural Center. It was on display through December 2013, and Arkansas resident and former Kansas City Monarch, Youngblood McCrary was on hand to open it up and close it out.

'Shades of Greatness' Exhibit Closes at Mosaic Templars Cultural Center

By Sandra McGrew
Updated: November 20, 2013, 8:00am

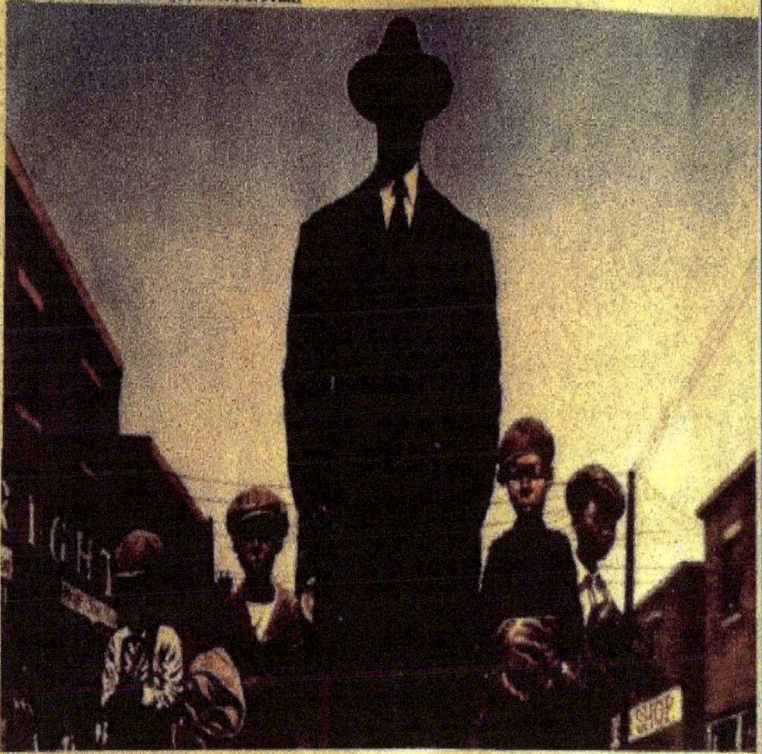

The Mosaic Templars Cultural Center "Shades of Greatness" exhibit marks its closing with a proper going away celebration this Thursday (Nov. 21) from 5:30p.m-7p.m. at the museum, 501 W. Ninth St., Little Rock.

"Shades of Greatness" is the first collaborative art exhibition inspired by the history of Negro Leagues Baseball. On loan from the Negro Leagues Baseball Musueum, the traveling exhibit features 34 original works by a host of national and regional artists, each of whom were given a detailed orientation to Negro Leagues history and challenged to produce works based upon their research and creativity.

The closing celebration will feature refreshments and guest speakers Bob Kendrick, President of the Negro Baseball Museum and William "Youngblood" McCrary, a former Negro Leagues player.

Pictured: A poster for the event

Bill, with daughter, Linda, in Little Rock, Arkansas

Bill signs hat for a fan.

Bill poses with a family at the event in Little Rock

Bill signs autographs for fans at the Mosaic Templars
Cultural Center.

Chapter 12: The Beloit Sports Hall of Fame

When something is meant to be, things just fall into place. A visit to a local restaurant, just outside the Hot Springs Village gates in Arkansas, a former police chief, named Richard "Dick" Thomas, of Beloit spotted a poster of Bill McCrary, and learned that Bill was a fellow Beloiter. This prompted a campaign for the induction into the sports hall of fame. And, he made it happen! Ironically, the Beloit Sports Hall of Fame is the same building where Bill attended Lincoln Junior High School, and received the largest "L" the school had ever given, and where his son Tracy is also on display for basketball.

Bill was inducted into the Beloit Sports Hall of Fame on June 5, 2014, to which he is much appreciative and thankful to Mr. Thomas for his determination, promptness, and persistence in handling this matter.

He said, "That night was one of the happiest, and proudest moments in my baseball history. The feeling of exhilaration and pride overwhelmed me, as I spoke to a group at the high school. It was just a moment I couldn't believe, and never thought I would live to see. It was grand! The event was scheduled to take place at the Hall of Fame, but they were inundated with reservations, so it had to be moved to the country club, which was equipped to seat more people. Of the 200-plus people who attended, 73 came on my behalf. They told me the event had to be moved because of the high number of guests attending for me. It really made me feel great. As a matter of fact, I was so elated, I couldn't contain myself. It has been a long time coming, and I am so blessed to have been able to see this day."

A teardrop fell, as Bill said, "My only regret is that my beloved Cleo isn't here to see, and to share in all of the good fortune and recognition I'm receiving because, as I said before, she is the reason for it all."

These articles are from The Beloit Daily News in Beloit, Wisconsin:

McCrary, 6 others to join Sports Hall

By Daily News staff | Posted: Tuesday, April 8, 2014 4:00 pm

In what is long overdue, William "Bill" McCrary's hometown will recognize him as one of its all-time athletic greats. McCrary, whose photo has hung in the Negro League Hall of Fame, is among the 2014 inductees into the Beloit Historical Society's Elliott-Perring Sports Hall of Fame.

McCrary will be on hand for the 29th Induction Ceremony at the Lincoln Center, 845 Hackett St., on June 5, along with fellow inductees: Don Zickert, John Schroeder, Chris Brown, Ty Talton, and Justin "Ace" Hanaman. Beloit Brewers/Snappers co-founder and long-time Midwest League President, George Spclius, will also be honored with the Bernie Barkin/Everett Haskell Lifetime Achievement Award.

McCrary was a sandlot star in Beloit, and played with several of the city's all-Black baseball teams before he signed with the Kansas City Monarchs. He was given the nickname "Youngblood" by then-teammate, Satchel Paige. He played with the Monarchs in 1946-47, then spent the rest of his baseball career with the semi-pro Omaha Rockets, as well as minor league teams of the New York Yankees and Chicago Cubs.

Hall of Fame event at Country Club

Posted: Wednesday, May 7, 2014 9:57 am

Ticket sales have been so brisk for the 2014 Beloit

Historical Society's Elliott-Perring Sports Hall of Fame Induction Ceremony that organizers have had to shift it from the Lincoln Center to the more spacious Country Club of Beloit.

The event will be held June 5.

The 2014 inductees include: William "Bill" McCrary, Don Zickert, John Schroeder, Chris Brown, Ty Talton, and Justin "Ace" Hanaman. George Spelius will also be honored with the Bernie Barkin/Everett Haskell Lifetime Achievement Award.

The award honoring Bill

Bill entertains friends.

Bill (3rd from left); Son Tracy (far right); Godson Jake (2nd from left); and son-in-law (left)

"I have to tell you this. While I was there, someone came up behind me and said, 'Bootch' McCrary. I thought to myself this has to be someone who knew me from a long time ago because nobody had called me that name since I was in school. I turned around and looked, and at first I didn't recognize who it was. When he told me his name, I immediately knew who he was. It was Dick McCauley, and it was so good to see him. We graduated together."

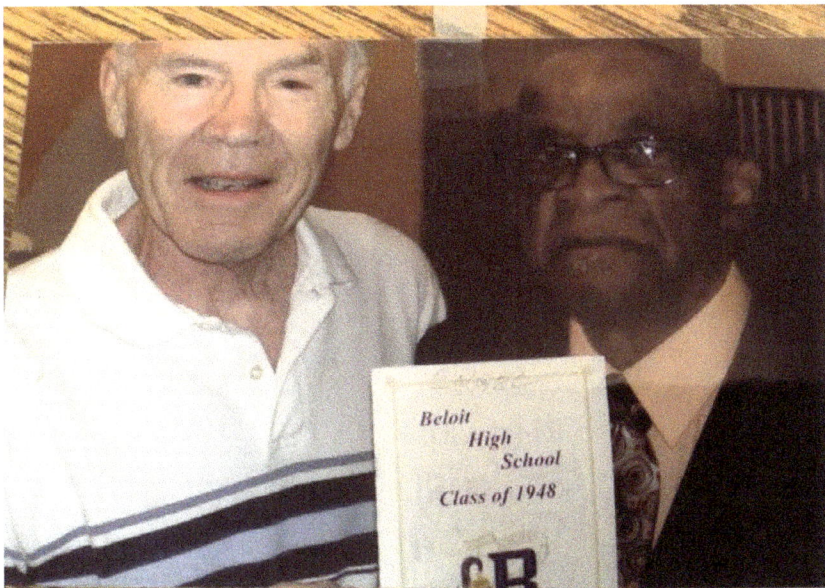

Bill and Dick McCauley pose for a photo together.

Bill delivers a speech at the induction ceremony.

Memorabilia on display at the induction ceremony.

A word of advice from a baseball legend:

Bill's advice to young people of today is to stay in school. He regrets not going on to college when he had the chance. A gentleman from Buffalo, New York offered him an opportunity to go off to college, but he didn't take it. Instead, his dream of playing baseball was the silver lining in the sky for him, so he ventured off in the pursuit of those dreams, and with the hope of becoming a major league player. He advises every youngster to go to school first, and then chase your dreams, or do both simultaneously.

SOURCES

James A. Riley, The Biographical Encyclopedia of the Negro Baseball Leagues, New York: Carroll & Graf Publishers, Inc. 1994.

Satchel Paige, Kansas City Monarchs, in *When the Game was Black and White* (New York: Abbeville Press, 1992), 84.

Negro Baseball League eMuseum

Baseballheritagemuseum.org

AFTERWORD

Most of the ball players of the Negro Baseball League have passed on, unfortunately; having never been recognized, and never fully realizing their dreams. They put their hearts and souls into playing the game, only to be disregarded, discounted, and disrespected. Those few, who did make it to the majors, encountered much discrimination, shame, and harassment. Some of them left; even after making it because they couldn't live under the pressure, and harsh treatment they had to endure.

They are all legends of the past, present, and future because many are seeking knowledge and information about these infamous human beings; who shared in making the game of baseball what is today. They brought a huge contribution to baseball, with their many styles of play and pitching, and their unique abilities, including: strength and their exceptional capabilities of running and stealing bases.

Some people dream of meeting a legend, at least once in life, while others live among them and don't know it. Some, like me, discover one in the family, accidentally. If it had not been for the research I was doing for this book, I may not have ever known about my cousin, Arthur "Superman" Pennington, who also played in Negro League Baseball. Thankfully, I was able to meet him this year, and hug a legend.

Legendary people are ordinary people, living ordinary lives. Most people will never meet, lay eyes on, or live in the presence of one, but unbeknownst to many in Hot Springs Village, Arkansas, we really do have...

A Legend Among Us.

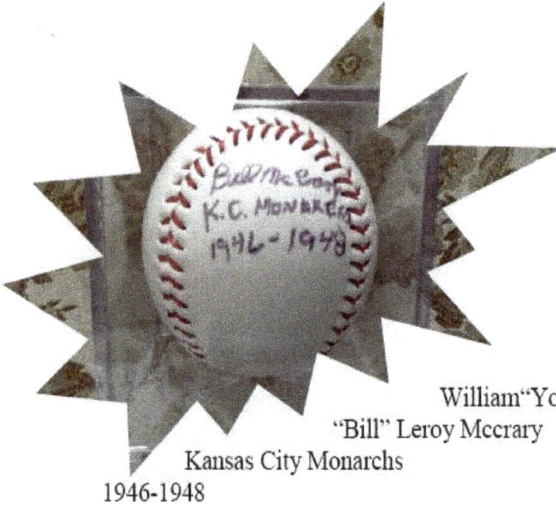

William"Youngblood"
"Bill" Leroy Mccrary
Kansas City Monarchs
1946-1948

This picture is courtesy of Linda Black. "I won this ball in an auction bid, at the Fellowship of Christian Athletes banquet in Hot Springs, Arkansas Summit Arena."

YESTERDAY'S BASEBALL

BILL Mc CRARY

Born in Beloit, Wisconsin
November 5, 1929
5' 10" - 170 lbs.

BILL Mc CRARY

Kansas City Monarchs
Negro Baseball League
1946-1948

PLAYED IN CHICAGO CUBS
AND YANKEES FARM SYSTEM.
PLAYED SHORT STOP
LIFETIME B.A. 341

Life is much like a book, each page representing another step along life's journey; each chapter being an added piece to the puzzle of life, and so it goes until the ultimate stage is reached: the conclusion of mortality.

Dreams don't always come true, but being in the driver's seat while chasing them makes for a whirlwind ride of excitement.

~~Linda Pennington Black

ABOUT THE AUTHOR

Author Linda Pennington Black grew up in Curtis, Arkansas; the fourth of twelve children. She received her early education via a one-room schoolhouse, and in many ways it was a blessing, as it exposed her to varying levels of education. She attended Peake High School in Arkadelphia, Arkansas. After graduating high school in

Chicago, Illinois, John Marshall Harlan, Linda relocated to Lansing, Michigan where she found employment with the General Motors Corporation. She was a faithful employee for over thirty years. While in Lansing, she chose Lansing Community College, as her institution of higher learning, where she was recommended for honors writing courses and became a valued member of the poetry club receiving the Associates of Arts degree. She went on to further her studies in psychology and criminal justice at the University of Phoenix.

Linda developed a love of writing early in her young life. At the tender age of 10, she wrote her first song. It was promptly sent off to Nashville to be set to music, and even though it was not published, Linda never lost sight of her love for writing. Her children's books include:

THE ADVENTURES OF BOOTS: THE GIANT SNOWBALL (Willow Moon Publishing), which won the publisher's MOONSTRUCK AWARD for best seller in 2011, **A PORPOISE FOR CARA** (Willow Moon Publishing), **S.T.O.P. BULLYING** and **MY DADDY IS A STAR**. Linda is also an award winning poet, with one of her works titled **THE DREAM/THE VICTORY** accepted by the White House, as a tribute to President Obama's first inauguration, and another published in the anthology **SISTAHS WITH INK VOICES.**

Linda and her husband Richard are proud to call six children, eleven grandchildren, and ten great-grandchildren...family. They reside in Hot Springs Village, Arkansas where Linda is an avid member of the Village Writer's

Club, a member of the National League of American Pen Women's local branch in Little Rock, Arkansas (where she helps coordinate and organize the Arkansas Writer's Conference), a member of her local church's choir and usher. She continues to write and still considers children to be her purest inspiration.